EXPERIENCING THE GOODNESS OF GOD

Virginia A. Romer, PhD

authorHOUSE®

AuthorHouse™
1663 Liberty Drive
Bloomington, IN 47403
www.authorhouse.com
Phone: 1-800-839-8640

First published by AuthorHouse 11/8/2010

ISBN: 978-1-4520-8772-6 (sc)
ISBN: 978-1-4520-8773-3 (e)

Library of Congress Control Number: 2010915804

Printed in the United States of America

Certain stock imagery © Thinkstock.

This book is printed on acid-free paper.

To my parents, Carlon & Stella Romer.

You have been my inspiration and shoulder to lean on. Not everyone is fortunate to have such wonderful parents. Ellsworth, Edward and I were among the blessed ones. Thank you for the wonderful family of which I am apart and for allowing me to experience God's goodness and love each day.

To Eduardo, my son.

From the day you were born, you have been the motivation needed to keep me going. You have made me the proudest mother ever and I love you dearly. Thank you for inspiring me to be a better mom, daughter, teacher and person.

Contents

Foreword

Dr. Leonard Johnson, author of "A – Z Inspirational Sayings" and President of the Bahamas Conference of Seventh-day Adventist saw the book as one that would grab the reader's attention.

In his words, "It is my pleasure to commend this short but touching account of one I have known most of my Adventist Church life as we belong to the same home church in Nassau, Bahamas –Johnson Park Seventh-day Adventist Church.

In my opinion, this work is a real, intriguing and relevant story about Ginny's life (Ginny is the way we her friends referred to her), written in a simple, candid and true-to-life style. Accordingly, it is bound to have an appeal to both adolescents and parents. Teenagers will find this book useful in dealing with some of life's problems and issues -be they the question of college studies, social relationships, financial responsibility and ultimate trust in God.

As for parents, they no doubt will see the need for understanding and forgiveness the way Christ does though hard at times.

I warn however, that once you begin reading this book you will find it difficult to put it down as it has a sense of suspense following each chapter leading one to the final chapter desiring to know the outcome or summary. Don't cheat by fast forwarding to the end instead enjoy each line, page and chapter of God speaking, intervening and blessing Ginny time and time again. Thereby, you will accord Him the privilege of blessing you through her experiences.

Essentially, I regard this account of Ginny's life as part one or incomplete believing that God is not finished with blessing her. I hope we will get a part two in what I believe could be a series of sort."

Introduction

"The act of putting pen to paper encourages pause for thought, this in turn makes us think more deeply about life, which helps us regain our equilibrium."

- Norbet Platt

When we come into this world, we do so not knowing what lies ahead for us. As life unfolds, we may find ourselves opening the right doors as well as the wrong ones. When we find ourselves in problems, we often ask 'Lord, why me?' We often forget that the Lord allows us to experience good and bad as a means of growth and helping us to realize that he is in control; something of which we need to be reminded once in a while.

No different from anyone else, my life has been one of good and bad experiences. Yet, as I reflect on my years, there is no doubt in my mind that God has been the play writer and director of my life. He has allowed things to happen that would help me grow both emotionally and spiritually.

From time to time during conversation, I have mentioned an event or two which occurred in my life, usually as a means of encouraging others. Surprisingly, the more I shared, the more persons would say to me that I need to write a book and share my experiences. I have always and still view myself as an ordinary person whose experiences were not unique, and I believe that many persons would be able to identify with. Sharing my life through prose was never something I had thought about doing, but since in Bahamian term the comment became a "scorched record", I decided to respond to the suggestion – hence this writing.

In this book, I will share with you 'The Goodness of God' played out in my life. It is my hope that you will be inspired not only to go after your personal dreams, but to allow God to lead in all areas of your life. You would not regret it.

Acknowledgments

The idea of writing a book came from friends who upon hearing of how God had been good to me in so many ways, thought I should put pen to paper and share my experiences. Although I had began to write, I took a long pause until I was nudged by Dr. Leonard Johnson, President of the Bahamas Conference of Seventh-day Adventist, who had recently published his first book. Thanks to his nudging, I returned to writing. This time, however, I took a different approach, writing my autobiography in the form of a motivational book.

Special thanks to Mr. Cedric Parker my attorney and dear friend for his guidance and editing of this book. His insight, suggestions and brainstorming sessions made the writing process smooth and productive.

This book shares with you aspects of my life from my childhood days to the present. In no way was this book written to make anyone mentioned to feel uncomfortable but to give a true picture of my life and the wonderful working of God.

My deepest thanks and gratitude goes to my family, especially my mother, for introducing me to Christ consequently enabling me to develop a relationship with him, thus experiencing and embracing his goodness every day.

CHAPER 1

A Humble Beginning

My God shall supply all your [our] need according to his riches in glory.

Philippians 4:19

I was born in The Bahamas on the island of New Providence, to parents who had not obtained a high school education. My parents, based on the mere fact that they did not complete school and the difficulty they endured making ends meet, thought it important that their three children recieved a good education.

Although strong church goers, my parents were not of the same religion. My father was Anglican while my mother was a Seventh-day Adventist. Who would have thought that the marriage of persons of different faith would stand the test of time, lasting for over fifty years? Although of different faith, they respected each other's religion. However, for my two bothers and me, it meant attending church both on Saturday and Sunday. By the time we reached the age of twelve, we were allowed to make our own decision and we all believed in and followed the Seventh-day Adventist faith. A faith in which two of us continue to be strongly active.

I grew up in a home that consisted of my father, mother, paternal grandmother, two brothers and me. My grandmother was a domestic worker, my father a licensed plumber while my mother was a homemaker. With my grandmother making just forty-five dollars per week and my father sometimes not bringing in anything at the end of the week, life was difficult. However, we were blessed to have a grandmother to whom God had granted the ability to budget and somehow stretch her small wage and be the provider for the family when at times my father brought in no money. Her sacrifices and budgeting enabled her to build a roof over our heads and an apartment building for extra income. How could one achieve all of this on a merger salary which had to stretch so far?

Since money was not always available, the thought of my brother and I obtaining a "good" education founded in my mother's religion, seemed an unobtainable dream. Yet, this was the dream and desire of my mother. Despite the difficult times, my parents and grandmother operating on faith, made the sacrifice to enroll my second brother and myself in a private school - Bahamas Academy of Seventh-day Adventists, to receive an education. My eldest brother was in the United States attending school, living with my aunt and uncle. Although back in those days fees were around fifty dollars and eventually increased, by my recollection to approximately one hundred dollars per term by the time I graduated in 1979, it was a challenge for my parents to pay.

Growing up as the daughter of a plumber, I had firsthand experience in watching both contractors and homeowners take advantage of my father whom they hired to work for them. If only my father was to collect the thousands of dollars owed to him to this day, then maybe he would be able to leave something for his grandchildren when he passes. Watching the pain my family went through having to experience once again "no show" of a contractor or homeowner who promised to drop off money that was owed, led me to make a personal commitment that at no time will I ask someone to work for me unless I already had the money put aside.

Fridays were often dreaded as we were never sure whether grocery money would come in or not. It seemed to a young child that disappointment came every Friday. Despite the many Fridays when no money came, we were able to have a meal. Often, we watched my mother and grandmother invent new dishes using whatever was available. Surprisingly, their 'unique meals' did not make us sick but rather provided us with a full stomach. This continuous experience allowed me to develop an appreciation for the simplest meal. I often spoke of these experiences with my son and nieces during their younger years.

Although blessings came during my childhood, thought was not given to them as coming from God but more so from my parents. After all, they were responsible for me. It is only after I became an adult and reflected on my own experiences, that in retrospect, I came to recognize the working of God in my life, during my childhood days.

CHAPTER 2

Opening of Doors

"The secret of getting ahead is getting started. The secret of getting started is breaking your complex overwhelming tasks into small manageable tasks, and then starting on the first one."

- Mark Twain

Where there is no vision, the people perish.

-Proverbs 29:18

When most adolescents are about to complete high school, they give thought to either furthering their education or entering the world of work. Indeed, it was the same for me. My mind was set on furthering my education. The school I attended, Bahamas Academy, was a strong promoter of tertiary education. To venture in such direction was quite costly in my circumstance as my parents did not have the funds. It was a dilemma staring me in the face. However, determination and faith eventually made my dream a reality.

In June 1979, with pride I graduated from Bahamas Academy with honors. Some twenty-six years later, in the month of May 2005, I walked across the stage of Pioneer Church at Andrews University in Berrien Springs, Michigan, the recipient of a PhD Degree in Curriculum and Instruction. Like many others, it had been a long journey, one with many bumps and detours. From time to time during this journey, I clearly saw the works of God and the outpouring of His blessings in my life.

After completing high school and not knowing where money would come from to further my education, I embarked upon finding employment. It did not take long for me to find a job. However due to my decision not to remain employed beyond a year, I did not take a glamorous job. A receptionist typist was the position I held at a Woodwork Shop, making seventy-five dollars per week. Determined to save, each week I deducted my tithes and offering which totaled ten dollars, and four dollars and fifty cents for a small medical insurance. The balance I placed in my savings account.

I often, at lunch time, wished I had kept enough money to purchase lunch rather than having to eat what was in my brown paper bag. Right across from my work place was a Kentucky Fried Chicken Restaurant which made the contents of my brown paper bag less appetizing. However, I constantly reminded myself of my goal and allowed it to lift my spirits. My work place was minutes away from a well known shopping area. When I wanted a change of scenery, I would take a stroll to the shops and browse knowing full well that my wallet was empty. This endless torture and self determination lasted for a year, at the end of which I had saved enough to pay for my first year and enrolled at Indian River Community College in Fort Pierce, Florida.

Words cannot describe the pride I felt purchasing my own airline ticket and having enough funds to pay my own tuition. My second brother and I both left for Florida to join my oldest brother in pursuit of further education. Things were going well, until we got the news that my eldest brother was considering moving to Atlanta with his wife. Upon hearing this, my mother made it very clear that we would not be returning to school, even though I was residing with my aunt and not my brother. Nonetheless, she stood by her decision and my brother and I had no other choice but to remain at home.

Can you imagine how depressed I was having now to remain at home and see my dream of obtaining a college education come to an end? I considered entering The College of The Bahamas, but I had not applied and was therefore unable to enroll the Fall Semester. Although all I thought about was going back to school, my father was keen that I should find a job and forget about college. I remained unemployed all of the 1981 Fall Semester but in February of the following year, my father found a job for me as a receptionist typist with a construction company.

The job was one I enjoyed, interacting with workers and clients. However, my heart was still set on going back to school. With an unyielding determination of being ready for the next Fall Semester, I submitted my application to The College of The Bahamas (COB) and commenced saving my funds. From the beginning I made my plans known to my boss and he was very supportive. My father, on the other hand, had his thoughts fixated on my continued employment and school was the last thing on his mind. Maybe it was because he did not want to have to think of finding tuition. However, never once did I plan to place my financial burden on him; yet I had no idea where the funds were coming from.

Although I had only saved tuition for one semester in September 1982, determined to go after my goal, I quit my job and enrolled at COB. The first semester was covered, yet I had no idea how I was about to pay for the Spring Semester. I was becoming anxious as registration was only a couple months away. I can recall saying out loud, "Lord where am I going to get the money for the next semester? I trust you to help me find a way." It was not long after, when once again, the Lord came through for me, opening doors.

It so happened that another student who majored in education like myself and who was now my new friend, in talking, mentioned that she was on the grant program. This was a program of which I knew nothing, and I learnt from her that the grant was available for Bahamian education majors with the stipulation that they maintain a certain grade point average. The Bahamas government, in an effort to attract more persons to the teaching profession, agreed to pay the tuition of students who majored in education while giving them a stipend twice a year to help with books and other supplies. Upon learning of this program, I found my way to the office and applied for the grant. Not only did I get it, but was also reimbursed the money I had paid for my first semester. I was suddenly rich! Indeed, God had sent my friend my way to share the information.

Have there been times when it seems nothing good is coming your way at all and then a number of good things come simultaneously? Well, it happened to me. One evening when I was working on school assignments, I received an unexpected phone call. Surprisingly, it was my former boss from the construction company calling to find out the schedule for my classes. He was offering me part-time work with hourly pay. Additionally, he was prepared to send the company car to collect me at the appropriate time. Not only was my school fees covered, but now I would be able to make and save additional monies. The Lord was indeed looking out for me. What had I done to deserve it? To this day, I cannot really say except I stayed focus with my church commitments, paying my tithes and offering and singing in the choir. I had not forgotten God during my educational journey.

For three years, I remained on the grant and held my part-time job. I maintained my grades and completed my studies in May 1985 with an Associate Degree and Teaching Certificate. That was only the beginning. With sufficient funds saved, I was able to begin classes toward my Bachelors at the College of Saint Benedict, St. Cloud Minnesota which offered an extension program in the Bahamas. There was no stopping me from going after my dream. I started the program a few months later in the summer of 1985.

Upon my graduating from COB, I was hired as a Language Arts teacher with the public school system. I finally had a steady income. This was important to me since I knew the cost of classes toward the Bachelor would be quite costly. Having a full work load and then having to attend classes in the evenings were challenging. However, I was comforted by the words "The Lord will never put on you more than you can bear". Although at times I felt frustrated, tired and ready to give up, I never did and in May 1989 I was able to brave the cold Minnesota temperature and matched for my degree with a pride that I cannot explain.

The cost of education looms over many and hinders them from accomplishing their personal goals. You would think that after getting my first degree I would be satisfied and focused on my career. Well, that was not to be. I still had in mind to go for yet another degree – my Masters. It would seem that the Lord was taking each step with me as once again He stepped in and sent His blessings my way.

I am so fortunate to belong to a religion that has colleges and universities worldwide and believes in educating while helping individuals to meet Christ or to develop a closer relationship with Him. The hand of the Lord was once again at work when He led the administration of Andrews University to have the foresight and vision to offer Christian education beyond the main campus, offering an extension program. As a result, a Masters Program in Education was brought to the Caribbean, and with a reduction in fees. This provided me with the opportunity to pursue my Masters in Education, specializing in Administration and Supervision. For four summers, instead of enjoying my vacation, I left the Bahamas with many other teachers and headed to Jamaica for classes. As a result, many Bahamians and Caribbean nationals were able to qualify themselves and do so for a cost within reach.

Having worked all year, the average teacher would be tired and in dire need of a vacation. To even think about enrolling in classes was ludicrous. Nonetheless, I took the plunge and ventured into my studies, emotionally drained and somewhat physically exhausted, but determined to go after my personal goal. Long hours of grueling classes, marathon chapters to be read for the next day, and being prepared for daily quizzes, not to mention none stop assignments, often caused the thought of giving up and making good use of a much needed vacation to cross my mind periodically. However, it was not to be for each time the thought came my way, the Lord would have someone to come into my life with the right thing to say. The devotions shared daily before the start of each class, did so much to keep me going. There is no doubt that it was the working of the Lord allowing just what I needed to hear, to be said.

Despite the many times I thought about quitting, I never did. The will power and strength came from the Lord. He provided me with the inner strength that I needed from time to time to keep going. Thanks to Him I persevered and made it through four summer sessions and a full semester, reaching the end. In May of 1994, I traveled to Michigan and marched with hundreds of others for the degree I always wanted.

As a teacher I have always maintained good relations with my students. As a result, I was often approached by them with personal situations seeking my advice. For some reason they were not comfortable with speaking to the Guidance Counselors of the school, so I became the next best thing. Not wanting to violate confidentiality, yet needing to give proper advice, I would often present hypothetical situations to the counselor seeking the best way to handle the situations. Due to the fact that so many students would share their problems, I decided to obtain proper training.

Having read earlier how I often thought about quitting my studies, the last thing you would have expected was to hear that instead of taking a break, I enrolled the following summer in another Masters Program in the hopes of eventually obtaining a doctorate in psychology. Andrews University had offered yet another extension program, this time in Trinidad. Two other Bahamians and I boarded the flight that took us to Trinidad to commence studies. Having done my first masters in Administration and Supervision, I had completed no courses that could be transferred towards a PhD in psychology. Knowing that I would have many courses to study, I decided to sign up to complete as many courses as I could, taking advantage of the reduced price. At that time courses on the main campus were more than four hundred dollars per credit. Where would I find such funds?

We were only able to complete one summer of classes in Trinidad when classes were moved to the campus in Michigan. However, the reduced price remained in place. In four summers, I was able to complete a Masters degree in Educational and Developmental Psychology. However, my hopes to continue diminished before my eyes for two reasons. Firstly, having attended a few doctorial defenses, I began to doubt my ability to handle the pressure and secondly, I saw no way in sight of affording full tuition price on campus. At best, I would only be able to take one course per summer which would then take me 'forever' to finish. Having given thought to my situation, I decided to give up on going after my doctorate in psychology and utilize my masters instead. With that degree, I would be more than qualified to work with high school students. Thus, I gave up on furthering my education, transferred from a Language Arts classroom teacher to a Guidance Counselor and began to focus on preparing for my son's departure to college which was only a few years away.

Despite the decision made, it would seem however that giving up on a doctorate degree was not to be for the thought continuously came to mind although I saw no financial way in sight. It was by chance that I found myself speaking with a friend who had completed the Master's program with me in Jamaica. It was then that I learnt that once again Andrews University was in the process of starting a Doctorate Program in Jamaica on the campus of Northern Caribbean University (formally West Indies College) at a reduced price. Upon hearing the news, I made contact to find out if there was any truth to what I had learnt and behold it was true. With hasty steps, I applied and was accepted to pursue a doctorate degree not in psychology, but rather in Curriculum and Instruction. Before the program was able to commence, news came where it could no longer be held in Jamaica and I would have to travel to the main campus in Michigan. The good news to this was that the price however, would remain the same. Talk about the goodness of the Lord coming my way once again! He had placed within my reach, my goal although in a new area, and at an affordable price.

Despite the work load and challenges that came with pursuing a doctorate while at the same time overseeing my son's studies, the Lord through His word and the encouraging words of church members, enabled me to stay focus even when I became discouraged and wanted to give up. In May 2005, I traveled to Michigan and with personal pride, marched for my degree. The tears were on the brink of spilling, but I held them in check. The Lord had indeed opened doors that enabled me to obtain firstly a 'Christian' education and secondly, the degree that I thought was out of my reach both ability and financially wise. There is no doubt in my mind that it was God who placed in the minds of Christian administrators at Andrews University, the vision to reach out to third world countries and provide quality Christian education at no doubt a financial lost to the university. Thanks to their listening to the still small voice of the Almighty, persons like me not only obtained quality education, are now better equipped to offer good service, but also more importantly, developed a closer relationship with the Father as a result.

CHAPTER 3

Speared Life

O give thanks unto the Lord for He is good for His mercy endureth forever.

- Psalm 136:1

Despite the educational success that was shared previously, my life did not go so smoothly. Shortly after beginning my first Master's in Jamaica, I had a near death experience. On December 23, 1991 I steered death in the eye but thanks to the goodness of God, my life was speared.

For a while, I had been involved in a relationship that in my view was 'perfect'. I was happy, in love and looking forward to a future with a wonderful man. However, little did I know that the relationship was not to be and that it would almost cost me my life. As Christians, we have been reminded repeatedly to seek God's direction and input in everything that we do. However, many like me choose to do things in their own way and that is where we make our biggest mistake. Not once did I seek God's guidance when it came to choosing my mate. As a result, I found myself with a wonderful person but with who came baggage that nearly cost me my life.

The love of my life and soul mate, whom in this book shall be called Lowell, was a wonderful individual. He was twelve years my senior but somehow we were perfectly matched. He was an educated person who was of the same profession as me. In fact, it was through our profession that we met. Our relationship was as such that we shared quality time together as a couple and as a family with my son. I could not have asked for a more understanding, devoted partner. There was never a doubt in either of our minds that we were loved by each other.

In September of 1987, I was headed to Minnesota to begin the last semester to completing my Bachelors Degree at the College of Saint Benedict. It was just before I was to leave that Lowell proposed to me, as he wanted to spend his life with no one else but me. After two years of knowing each other but only one year of an actual relationship, I accepted the proposal. I left for college with mixed emotions as I was happy to be engaged, to finally be at the end of my degree but sad to be leaving my family and fiancé behind. Little did I know that placing the ring on my finger was to bring about turmoil that would almost cause me my life.

Upon my completion of the semester, I returned home only to be faced with a great deal of unpleasant phone calls, messages and some stalking. It seems highly unlikely to find a man now a day that did not have a child or two even though he may not be married. In my desire to trust my partner and not being one to investigate as such, I took him at his word that he was divorced and had three children. I did not have a problem with this because I knew that very few men in his age bracket would not have been married before. However, what I came to learn that lead to almost losing my life was that the divorce had not been finalized and that the wife was still living in hope that they would resolve their differences and get back together.

Being a church goer, the wife did not believe in divorce and in fact, had no intension of allowing Lowell to receive one. I learnt after the fact that it was her nature ever since their separation, to find out about any relationship he was involved in and make herself a nuisance to the person, resulting in a breakup. This time, I was the target. At first, I exercised patience as Lowell worked through finalizing his divorce. However, as time went by and every court date was somehow postponed; after receiving numerous unpleasant phone calls; after learning from family and friends on how they were approached by the wife; with the final straw being administrators at my school contacted in the hopes of finding out information that would lead to the lost of my job; I had reached my limit and had no other choice but to end the relationship. It was then that I had a near encounter at death's door, only to have the Almighty think me worthy of a second chance. Here's my story.

It was a Monday afternoon and at the time, my church was in a crusade. After venturing down my own path for a while, I had finally decided to get back on track and give my life to the Lord. In fact, the decision had already been made for the upcoming baptism which was to be held that Saturday. I needed to make a dash by Lowell and then head home to prepare for service.

A few days earlier, I had contacted Lowell and had arranged to pass by his home to collect his contribution to the credit card bill that had incurred while we were together. If I said I had not missed him, I would have lied. I looked forward to seeing him despite the fact that the relationship was over. We took the opportunity to catch up on what had happened with each other over the past weeks. Having an enjoyable conversation and both of us not wanting it to end,

I was invited to accompany him to pick up some drawings from a friend. I did not have a problem with going so long as I would be back in time to get dress for the evening service.

The drive was quite a pleasant one that I was very much at ease. Little did I know that the drive was a means to get me alone and away from everyone. The drive took us to the western outskirts of town in a secluded area where houses were few and far apart. Lowell stopped the car and from under his seat, pulled out a handgun. I cannot begin to describe the fear that came upon me instantly. Never before in my life had I seen a gun other than in pictures and on television. In seconds my life flashed before my eyes and I thought my time had come.

Although I tried to reason with him and say all the things I thought he wanted to hear, it turned out to be a waste of my time. I cannot say when the gun was fired as I did not see him pull the trigger nor did I hear the shot. I can only recall regaining consciousness and feeling something dripping down the side of my face. It was only when I touched my face and looked at my fingers did I see blood and realized what had occurred.

For what seemed like hours, we drove around with me going in and out of consciousness. Each time I became alert, I would enquire as to where we were going and each time the destination changed – hospital, home, my parents. Yet I ended up at none of those places. I can recall the last time, upon noting our location, I enquired as to where we were going, and the gun was placed at my side. It was then that I realized he himself did not know what was to happen next and it would be in my best interest to keep my mouth close.

After riding around for some time and wanting to confirm whether I was dead or not, he attempted to feel for my pulse. Having problem locating a pulse, the inside lights were turned on during which time I held my breath. Not seeing my chest moving must have convinced him that I was dead; hence I was removed from the car and left for dead in the bushes.

However, my work here on earth was not to come to an end so quickly. The Lord granted me a clear mind and sufficient strength to hold on to nearby trees hoisting myself up. As I made steps, I felt like a drunken woman staggering from side to side. My head was dizzy, I was weak and all I really wanted to do was sleep. Through all the haziness in my head, I had enough sense to recognize car lights and the direction in which they were headed. Thanks to the lights, I was able to slowly make my way from the bushy area to the main road and place myself in the middle of the dark road to ensure that a driver was sure to see me. It had to be the work of the Lord to send a police car my way in just a few short minutes. The officers stopped, called in the situation, and proceeded to take me up town to the hospital.

Examination by the doctor revealed that the bullet had lodged in the left temple with fragments over the left side of the brain. The ear drum had been severely damaged which should have affected my balance. In fact, the doctor was somewhat surprise to learn that I was able to stand upright and walk out of the bushes. In his view, I should have lost my balance and not be able to walk. With the Lord on my side, I overcame the odds. Although the larger portion of the bullet was removed without surgery, surgery was needed to remove the fragments.

If I was to say that I was not afraid, I would be lying. Having been told of the importance of removing the fragments which could result in serious infection, I knew the surgery had to be done. Yet, I was afraid of something going wrong. After all, the fragments were on the brain. The good thing was the surgery called for entry from behind the ear. The doctor was able to cut behind the ear, flip it over and access the fragments. There was no shaving of the head, which should have been the least of my worries, but yet, a typical woman's concern.

Although I did my best to remain in a cheery mood, I was afraid. It is so funny how we make promises to God when we find ourselves in life threatening situations. I was no different. As I sent up my silent prayers, I made a promise to serve Him. As I was rolled down the corridor, I can recall humming every hymn I could remember from the church hymnal. For the second time in a short space of time, my life flashed before my eyes. Would I survive the surgery? I was truly afraid that I may not have awoken.

I serve an awesome God who not only brought me through the surgery but also allowed me a speedily recovery. You see, Christmas was right around the corner and I had no desire to spend this festive time in the hospital. On the day that I was admitted to the hospital, I shared a room with two other females each of us having surgery on the same day by the same doctor. Their surgery however, was nowhere as severe and risky as mine. Within the short time shared, we had become close and we all vowed to leave the hospital together. Plans we had made without consulting the doctor.

I was the last of the three to have surgery that day. By the next day, the doctor was able to indicate to the others when he would be releasing them. In his view, I had at least another week in the hospital. This was not something I wanted to hear so I pressed him to reveal under what condition he would let me go home. Once again he was concern about my balance, dizziness, headaches and fever. I needed the Lord to intervene and allow me to go home. I needed Him to show the doctor that all was well with me. I sent up a silent plead.

My determination to be released led to my constantly nagging the doctor during his rounds. I finally got him to agree that should I have no dizziness and be able to walk a straight line showing my balance was stable, he would consider releasing me. Surprisingly, when the doctor did his examination he was amazed by my ability to walk with no indication of problem with balance. With a host of phone numbers and my assurance that I would contact him at the slightest dizziness or lost of balance, I was released from the hospital three days after the surgery. What a miracle! I would be spending Christmas with my family.

Once again, God in His goodness speared my life allowing me to survive firstly the gunshot to the head and secondly, major surgery. Although I have lost total hearing in my left ear, have nerve damage to the left side of my face, and have lost my once beautiful smile, I am just happy that my life was speared and that I am alive. Thank you God for loving me so much that you gave me a second chance at life.

CHAPTER 4

Forgiveness

For if ye forgive men their trespasses, your heavenly Father will also forgive you. But if ye forgive not men their trespasses, neither will your heavenly Father forgive your trespasses.

- Matthew 6:14, 15

Having been near death's door by the hands of another for the average person may bring hatred and a desire to see that that individual is incarcerated for life. The last thing you would expect to hear much less see is the victim visiting the assailant. However, it was just the opposite with me. There was this strong desire for me to see Lowell, my assailant. Despite what he had done to me, he was my love and his actions were outside of the norm. I needed to see him. I needed to talk to him. I needed to make sure that he was alright. I therefore went on a frenzy to find out how to obtain a prison visit.

After making my inquiries, I leant I had to wait until the beginning of the next week to gain access to Her

Majesty's Prison. There were many persons gathered at the gate waiting for the name of their relative or friend to be called. The names were called in alphabetical order and the letter 'M' which began his surname, seemed further than it actually was in the alphabet. After what seemed like forever, I finally heard Lowell's name and it was then that I learnt that not only was I there to see him, but also a cousin of his he had always spoken so fondly about and whom I had met on a few prior occasions. Together we entered the gate, underwent our body search and then followed the path to Maximum Security Block.

The unpleasant stench from the prison filled my nostrils as I neared the building. The steers of inmates congregated in the yard or at iron bar windows was quite uncomfortable. Despite second thoughts filling my mind, I knew I had to continue; I had to see Lowell. The visiting area was as such that a screen separated inmates from their guests. We took our seats and awaited the arrival of Lowell.

When I saw the man that I loved take his slow dazed walk toward us, I was overwhelmed with grief and the tears flowed. To be honest, the entire visiting session was one of tears. I steered and cried; words were lodged in my throat unable to exit. However, Lowell somehow managed to say a few words thanks to his cousin who in my view was sent by God to be there for that meeting. Somehow, she found the right words to say to both of us. It had been a visiting session I would never forget. It was there and then that I knew I had no animosity towards Lowell, despite what he had done. I knew it was important for me to forgive him as much as it was important for him to be told he was forgiven. Having expressed my forgiveness, I left there feeling at peace with myself.

When I had been released from the hospital, I was unable to sleep without replaying in the mind the entire shooting ordeal. Complete darkness had always been the most comfortable way for me to sleep, yet I had to keep the lights on. Well, my sleeping problem came to an immediate halt upon my return from my visit. Somehow my inability to sleep had been connected to my need to know how Lowell was doing. That night, I slept like a baby. It was the first night since the ordeal that I had gotten a good night's sleep.

In the Bible, we have been told repeatedly to love one another and to forgive. However, it is hard to determine if we would truly be able to do so in adverse circumstances. It is only when we find ourselves in such a situation that we will truly learn from within whether we can truly forgive or if our forgiveness depends on the situation. Like most individuals, it was highly unlikely that it would be easy for me to forgive someone who almost took my life, yet I found it very easy to do.

My forgiveness extended to my writing a letter to the prosecutor expressing my wish for no charges to be brought against Lowell. However, my wish could not be considered and this was communicated to me in a letter from the Attorney General's office. Despite the reality that the case had to be tried, I had made the decision not to turn my back on him. My decision to assist him as best I could was for as much my healing as his. It was important in my view that Lowell had less to concern himself with, so I decided to handle as much of his personal affairs as I could. These included taking care of outstanding bills and finding funds for his legal expenses; not to mention getting messages to family members. At the end of the day, Lowell was convicted and sentenced to five years in prison.

During that period, I visited him monthly, took Christmas dinner on Christmas day and ensured that he and his cellmate had the necessary toiletries. At no time did I turn my back on him. When I was unable to visit, we communicated through letters, poems and drawings. For both of us emotional healing came. Having committed my life to Christ days just prior to the shooting, I was looking at things differently. My willingness to extend a helping hand and communicate not only made things a little more bearable for Lowell, but also put both of us on the road to emotional healing.

Despite my willingness to forgive, it was very difficult for members of my family, especially my mother. A true test of our Christianity comes in circumstances such as this one. When we confess to be a Christian, we never can tell how we would react. Understandably, human components take over and naturally we develop hatred and an instant desire to get even with the one who has wronged us. Yet as Christians we are asked to forgive and turn the other cheek. When I sort to do that, many thought me crazy or stupid. However, I must say that there were those who admired me for my ability to forgive. I sometime wonder, however, if my reaction would have been the same if my assailant was a complete stranger. I cannot honestly answer that at this time and I hope I am never put in the situation to find out. I can only hope that Christ's forgiving love has somehow rubbed off on me that I too would be able to forgive the wrongdoings of another whom I had no previous knowledge or relationship.

CHAPTER 5

Ongoing Goals

O taste and see that the Lord is good: blessed is the man that trusteth in Him.

- Psalm 34:8

"You are never too old to set another goal or to dream a new dream."

- C. S. Lewis

As one journeys through life, there should always be ongoing goals that one wishes to accomplish. Accomplishing any goal calls for planning. However, there are times despite our planning when our goals seem unobtainable, yet we venture out in faith hoping that somehow the end result would materialize. Putting myself through school in its self was a challenge and although I did not always know how I was going to reach the end, I stayed focus and pursued my education to the very end.

Obtaining my education was not the only personal goal I wanted to achieve. There were others and not surprisingly, they came to pass. Earlier in the book, I failed to mention that during my final year of teacher training at College of the Bahamas, I found myself pregnant. Just three weeks before I began my teaching career and two months short of turning twenty-three, I gave birth to my son Eduardo. Being single and just starting a new career, there is no doubt that what happened should not have occurred. Additionally, I had gone against all of my upbringing and had violated the sanctity of marriage, having a child for a married man.

In deed my actions were wrong and I had brought hurt and embarrassment to my family, especially my mother. For quite some time my mom would not speak to me. She was understandably angry, hurt and disappointed. A few weeks passed whereby we walked throughout the house as if each were not there. Surprisingly, one Sunday afternoon upon returning from a visit to her sister, my mother actually spoke to me. I was totally surprised and eventually learnt that my aunt Rose who we affectionately called Mama Rose, was responsible for the change.

Being the only girl and last child, my mom and I were quite close. It was upon this premise that my aunt had convinced her to make amends our relationship as I, out of the three children, would be the one most likely to stand by her side through sickness or any other misfortune. To say that the relationship resumed as though nothing had happened would be an understatement. However, in time it was mended. My mom extended her assistance throughout the pregnancy. She went with me on a shopping spree for the baby and assisted in planning a surprise baby shower. Although she would have preferred things to be different, the reality was what it was and she did her best to help me. Upon the birth of my son, my mother claimed him as her own. Even today some twenty four years later, my son is not my son, he belongs to my parents. The love that exists between them is deep. Their relationship is one that

I have chosen to accept even though at first I found myself somewhat jealous.

Nonetheless, my son was here and regardless of the fondness my parents had for him, he was still my responsibility. I was determined to equip myself with the tools needed to provide for my son and myself. Obtaining my degree was one such tool. Attending classes and caring for a young child was not easy. However, thanks to the support of my parents, especially my mother, I was able to leave my son in their care and attend evening classes. My parents not only assisted with my son but knowing what I was trying to accomplish, allowed me to live under their roof while refusing to accept any financial contribution to the monthly expenses. My father just wanted me to go after my dream. However, my conscience would not allow me to avoid contributing. There were times when money was slow in coming. These were the times I would slip a few dollars to my mom, as she was the one who paid the bills. There was the understanding that when my father got around to giving her the money to pay the very same bill, the money was hers to keep and spend on her. This was our little secret for quite some time.

Unlike many young mothers today that turn over the responsibility of their children to grandparents, I took seriously my role of being a mother. My son was indeed my responsibility, since every step I took was with him in mind. When I was leaving for Minnesota to complete my last semester at The College of Saint Benedict, I ensured that financial provision was made for him.

All along I was able to pay my tuition from my pocket as studying part-time made things easier. Now, I had to complete my final semester on campus and this called for more money than I had. I needed a loan. Obtaining a loan for my last semester was not easy. The bank was requesting a letter from The Ministry of Education (my employer) stating that upon my return I would still have a job. For some reason the letter was not forthcoming and so I had to rethink what action to take. Using another financial institution and deliberately not revealing that I was going to school but rather that I needed financial assistance to purchase furniture in the United States for my parents' home, I was able to obtain the money needed. Yes, I had told a deliberate lie. At the time, it was the only way I saw the money being loan to me. Otherwise, I did not see my final semester on campus within reach.

I cannot say the Lord helped me in obtaining the loan as I am sure He did not appreciate the lie I told. At the time, I saw my honesty as a hindrance to achieving my goal. My honesty had prevented me from obtaining the loan from the first institution approached. Back then, I had never given thought to that fact that maybe I was not to go at that time, nor was I exercising faith as I should trusting God to work things out. The completion of my degree was a mere four months away. It was time for me to go and in my view nothing was going to stand in my way.

Ensuring that my bills were covered even while I was away was of utmost importance to me. After careful planning and budgeting, I left sufficient funds with my mother to make the monthly financial payments to the bank for the duration I would be away as my salary would cease for that period. I also left ample funds to pay for my son's tuition and provide food for him even though I knew my parents would ensure that he ate. I just knew he was my responsibility and did not want my parents to be burdened in any way.

Upon my return, I continued to view my son as totally my responsibility even though we were still residing with my parents. After seven years of living with my parents and putting myself through school, I realized it was time for me to provide a home for my son and me. So, I made an appointment with a lending institution to find out, based on my salary, how much I would qualify for. Once I had obtained this information along with all documents I would have to submit, my next task was to locate a company that was offering a package deal. As luck would have it or rather as God had led, the construction company for whom I had worked and maintained a good relationship, was offering packages – lot and house together.

I met with them, shared what I had qualified for and sought to find out if they had a package that would fit my budget. Although I had always known I was appreciated when I worked for the company, it was not until I approached them about a home that I truly knew how much. Despite the fact that the company wanted to make a decent profit from the deal, they also wanted to help me in any way that they could and indeed they did. The price of my package was reduced significantly with them making minor profit from the transaction. Our wonderful working relationship had paid off and I was reaping the benefit.

At the time I wanted to get my house, the lending institution which gave the lowest interest rate had temporarily put a hold on lending. Despite this, I was determined. I wanted to ensure that my documents were in place and hopefully I would be at the top of the list. Therefore, I did everything that needed to be done, submitting everything and calling from time to time to find out if the freeze on lending had been lifted. By the time lending resumed, I think my name was quite known. It was therefore, no surprise when the call came and I had a month to take in my down payment and closing cost.

I should mention that when I had put the house building in motion, not one penny had been saved. However, once I knew what was required of me, I borrowed money from the

Credit Union and placed the full amount on a monthly fix awaiting the call. It is not the norm for someone to borrow their down payment but to have saved it. Nonetheless I did and when the call came, with pride I signed my name on the line committing myself to a thirty year mortgage.

In December 1994, nine years and three months after the birth of my son, we moved into our cozy home which we named Villa Tranquila – Home of Tranquility. We took up residence with only the bare necessities – fridge, stove, bedroom set, computer table, and a bookcase. In my son's room was a folding cot for a bed, a dresser and a study desk for homework. My mother provided us with used drapes for the windows and a few dishes while my grandmother had treated my son to the bookcase, dresser and study desk. Although the furnishing was sparse, I was just happy to be in my own home, providing for my son and myself. My son did not share my excitement. He was leaving the only home he had known and the grandparents who he adored and looked forward to going home to. I just knew it was time for mother and son to venture out on their own. The Lord, once again, had allowed me to achieve yet another goal.

CHAPTER 6

Making ends met

But my God shall supply all your [my] need according to his riches in glory by Christ Jesus.

- Philippians 4:19

Moving into my own home had greatly affected my finances. My son had always attended a private school and at that time was attending Queen's College, one of the top private schools in the Bahamas. Yes, despite the fact that I had benefited from Adventist education, I had no plans to send my son to my former school. While in high school, many of us had issues with the strict rules and had vowed never to send our children there. In fact we had named our school 'The Pink Prison' with our principal as the warden and the teachers as prison officers. However, I must be honest and share that it was the view of many graduates that our alma mater was not producing the kind of results on the national exams as the other private schools. This was just another reason to send our children elsewhere.

Finding tuition after obtaining a mortgage had become

a challenge and so I had to make a decision. Despite my personal views of my school, I moved my son and placed him at my alma mater - Bahamas Academy, which too was a private school but was less expensive. It was still a challenge for me to find the funds when tuition was due. I needed to make extra money.

Teaching was not only my career but my love. I decided to take the opportunity to make extra money using my professional skills. I sent out my resume' to a number of evening institutes in search of an evening job teaching English Language. At first I heard nothing then I got a call from none other than Bahamas Academy Evening Institute. However, they were not looking for an English teacher, but a typing instructor. According to my resume', I had held typing jobs and so I was asked about teaching the class. Although I had no certificates in typing, I had taken the course in high school and was quite good at it. I accepted the challenge, got a hold of a typing book and got my hands on examination papers for which I was to prepare my students. I threw myself into my classes and was pleased when my students year after year passed the Pitman exam out of England, many with first class passes.

After about two years of teaching typing classes, I was also asked to teach English Language classes. For nine years I worked at the evening institute and for the entire time, every penny was used to pay my son's school fee. You see, I was paid at the end of each term. I would cash the check at one bank and cross the street to deposit it at another. The money may have stayed in my hand each time not more than about fifteen minutes, depending on the queue in the second bank. In deed I was living the saying "Pay today, broke today." It was ironic that the evening school closed just when my son was graduating. The Lord had once again opened a door and kept it open to ease my financial burden for the duration it was needed.

Having moved into my home with the bare necessities, I needed to make additional money to properly furnish it. Being one who loved working and who had goals to achieve, I was provided with and accepted the offer to make extra money with the Ministry of Education (my employer) through the writing of English papers for the Bahamas Junior Certificate Examination (BJC) and the marking of English papers for the Bahamas General Certificate of Secondary Education Examination (BGCSE).

Each time I wrote or marked, I would designate the money for things to be done in my house. Slowly but surely, I fenced my yard, fully furnished and carpeted my house and made additional home improvements. No one could convince me to use the money for anything else. Jokingly, my home was given the name 'The BJC House' by a few of my coworkers. Not only did I make enough money to furnish my house, but I was able to save enough to pay my tuition each summer when I traveled in pursuit of my master's and doctorate degrees.

It has been fifteen years and seven months since I moved into my home. My recent check on the mortgage showed that with my present monthly payment, I would complete my mortgage within four and a half years, knocking off ten years. It seems like just yesterday I moved into my home, yet fifteen years have passed and within four and a half years I would be debt free. I cannot tell you how great I feel and I owe it all to the Almighty who has stayed with me every step of the way.

As parents we look forward to our children completing high school hoping to ease our financial burden yet in many instances such a burden is just beginning. If it is your goal to provide your children with a college education, then you should plan in advance. Upon the birth of my son, I took out an education policy with Heritage. Having to pay the bills single handedly that would normally be shared by couples; I could not pay into the policy as much as I would have liked. I just knew I needed to have something in place to assist my son when the time came.

Having both parents in the life of a child is ideal and what all should aspire for. Of course this is most often assured when children are born within the sanctity of marriage, which was not the case with my son. However, I must say that my son's father did his best to be in his life. Each summer my son would spend time with his father, stepmother and siblings developing a relationship. However, having a family of his own, his financial contribution was small and really did very little to help me. Nonetheless, I gladly accepted what he gave and deposited it each time to my son's bank account.

My son's father has always supported me in my quest for my various degrees. He was the one person who had encouraged me to go for my doctorate. When I gave thought to pursuing that degree, I had to consult him as I did not want my studies to interfere with my son going straight into college upon graduating from high school. The education insurance that I had taken out matured when my son turned eighteen. However, my son was graduating at the age of sixteen, two months short of turning seventeen. I knew that I would need the assistance of his father. From our discussion, the agreement was made that our son would live with him in Nashville Tennessee and attend school at a community college for the first two years and that he would be responsible for the tuition. It was only because of this agreement that I enrolled in the doctorate program.

Everything went well with my son living with his father and attending school. His father had taken out a student loan for which he was to be responsible. After two years, my son completed the community college and got his Associates Degree. At the end of his second year of college, I had completed my doctorate and the insurance was available to pay his school fee. He then transferred to Tennessee State University to complete his Bachelor's in Accounts and I took over responsibility for his tuition. Throughout his entire time at school, I was responsible for travel expenses. Upon change of school, I was also responsible for textbooks. I found that the money from the insurance was only enough to pay tuition. I had to personally find money for all other expenses. Thank goodness another door opened and I made extra money teaching for the Technical Cadet Program, two afternoons per week.

The Technical Cadet Program is a program put on by the Ministry of Education in conjunction with private companies promoting technical careers. Although students were exposed to technical areas, they still had to be taught math and English and that is where I came in. I was able to help students with their English while helping myself financially. The money made from this venture was air marked for my son and his college expenses. Should you have or would have had a child in college you would agree that there was always a call or email asking for money. Seldom did a call come without the attachment of "Mommy I need you to send me some money". I loved hearing from my son, but I always waited for the shoe to drop.

Therefore, you can imagine how happy I was when graduation became a reality rather than a longing. In December of 2006 I traveled to Tennessee and sat with my son's family – father, stepmother, siblings and nephews and watched with pride as he received his degree. I was even more overwhelmed knowing that thanks to the Almighty, I had done it. The school was owed no money and my headache of paying tuition was over. My son had made the decision not to pursue an MBA but to return to the Bahamas and concentrate on becoming a CPA (Certified Public Accountant). He was indeed unique as most Caribbean persons having US Citizenship would jump at the opportunity to remain in the US, but not my son.

Having paid school fees since my son was two years old you can imagine, therefore, how I felt at graduation. However, that joy was short lived when I learnt that the student loan that was taken out by my son's father was still outstanding. You must understand that I am one who believes in clearing my bills. Therefore, I was quite upset to learn that two years had passed and only one payment had been made to the loan. When I consulted my son's father regarding the matter, I was angered when I learnt that he had no intention of paying off the bill. If financial difficulty had been cited as the reason for not paying the bill, I would have understood and automatically offer to assist. However, the reason given angered me so much so that I think the entire settlement of Tarpum Bay, Eleuthera where I lived must have heard me as I fussed on the phone.

He was refusing to pay the bill due to the fact that our son had made the decision not to pursue his MBA. He felt Eduardo should pay the bill himself. This infuriated me since as parents we had agreed to provide him with his first degree, something both of our parents were unable to do for us. In my case it would have been something my parents no doubt would have done if they had the resources. It was then that I knew I would have to be the one to free the debt. I had made a promise to my son and myself that I was determined to keep. As an individual knowing how difficult it was for me to obtain my degrees, I had made a promise to my son and myself upon his birth that I would ensure that he got his first degree. There was no way I was going back on my promise. A promise is a promise and for the last time, I would take responsibility for my son.

Three months prior to my son's college graduation, I was promoted to Vice Principal of a high school and relocated to the island of Eleuthera. This move resulted in my losing out on all the extra money I made through my evening jobs. No such work was available on the island when I first arrived. There was no way my salary was going to help me in clearing this bill. What was I to do? Where was the money to come from? Would I have to take out a loan? Then something happened. I got word that the Bahamas Technical and Vocational Institute (BTVI) for adults out of Nassau, was establishing an extension program in Eleuthera. Could this be the answer to my financial dilemma?

Surprisingly, I had applied to the same institution for a part-time job at least a year prior and had gotten no response and just days before I got my promotion, had received the call asking me to teach part-time. At the time of the call I had confirmed my willingness to teach but in a matter of days, had to contact them informing them of my move to Eleuthera. Ironically, it was the same institution coming to the island and once again the opportunity to work for the institution was before me. Was this pure luck or what? Could this be my golden opportunity? Without hesitation, I made contact and got the job. For a year and a half, I taught for the institution and the salary made was used to pay off the student loan. Shortly after the loan had been paid, the institution discontinued classes in all the Family Islands due to financial difficulty. Was it the working of the Lord that the institution came along when it did, providing me with means to clear my debt? There is no doubt in my mind that God played a key role in the way things turned out and I am forever grateful.

CHAPTER 7

Ongoing blessings

"As much as we need a prosperous economy, we also need prosperity of kindness and decency."

- Caroline Kennedy

It is more blessed to give than to receive.

- Acts 20:35

The blessings that we sometime experience may in part be due to the things we did out of the goodness of our heart. This is something I truly believe and have seen manifested throughout the lives of my parents and now myself. Although I grew up in a poor family, my family was free in their sharing with others. My mother could be found tending her backyard garden, and often shared limes, plums, peas and hands of bananas with the neighbors. She loved baking and once again she would share cakes and pies with friends, church members or neighbors.

My grandmother, on the other hand, was devoted to

her church. She supported financially many of the building projects and other ventures such as the purchasing of pews. There were many times when she would contribute to someone's medical cookout or education funds. My parents' and grandmother's love and willingness to share with and assist others brought many blessings upon them. Somehow doors were opened just when they needed to be and my parents were able to meet their financial commitments. The attributes of sharing and giving of oneself was passed on to my siblings and me.

We have been instructed by God to do unto others as we would have them do unto us. Hence it seemed so right to extend a helping hand to others without expecting something in return. When I attended COB, my typing skills came in very handy. I was able to type all my papers and the papers of friends. Although I could have used some money, I could never bring myself to charge anyone. Considering I provided paper, did the typing and corrected the grammar, many would say I was overly generous. I should have made a financial killing, but rather I collected "thank you's". Maybe I should have made a financial killing, but I would like to think in retrospect that I was extending the hand to others that God extends to each of us every day. For me, just knowing that I was able to help someone was payment enough.

At COB, I made a number of friends. There was one who was not a Bahamian and therefore had to pay higher tuition fees. She was married and had two sons. Unfortunately, her husband died and she was forced into being the sole provider for her family. This resulted in her having to discontinue her studies and seek employment. I had just completed teaching practice when I met her in a store and learnt of her plight. My natural instinct to help her went into action without a second thought. Right there and then, I committed myself to helping her out financially so that she could complete her studies and be in a better position to support her sons. Today she is a teacher, and in spite being a single parent, she was able to put her sons through college. Each time I see her and hear about the success of her sons now married and each with a family of their own, I am happy to know that I played a small part in their lives.

When I became a teacher, I did not limit myself to my classroom duties, but got involved in many extracurricular activities. One activity was that of cheerleading. I found myself being competitive, and wanting the cheerleaders to do well so I pulled out all the stops. It was not a surprise when I found myself using the sewing skills that my mother had passed on to me to make uniform for the cheerleaders of the sports house I coordinated and not charging a dime. I remember on one occasion having twenty four skirts to sew and soliciting my mother's help. Despite the electricity used, we did not charge a penny. In my opinion, it was enough challenge for the girls to purchase the material much less paying to have them made. I have always tried to be considerate of others which by some may be seen as a down fall. It was nice just knowing that I was able to decrease the financial burden of students and help some to be cheerleaders who might otherwise not have been.

The ability to reach out to someone for assistance is not easy for many. I am one of those individuals. No matter how difficult things may get, I could never ask anyone outside of immediate family members to help me. However, I am more than willing to lend a helping hand to someone in need wherever I could. The simple task of transporting an individual is something I never hesitate to do even when the gas is low and money is scarce and with the recent recession, it has been scarce indeed. I remember once speaking with a friend who said to me that if she had to take someone anywhere, including her own mother, the person had to put gas in her car. I have often listened to persons who seem to do nothing without pay and have heard of the financial problems they have often faced. Somehow they seem not to know that God blesses us when we bless others.

For those of you who may be experiencing financial difficulty, it could be because of your lack of willingness to give of yourself expecting nothing in return. On the other hand, could it be because you do not give back to God that which is His? In Malachi 3:8, 9 it reads "Will a man rob God? Yet ye have robbed me. But ye say, wherein have we robbed thee? In tithes and offerings. Ye are cursed with a curse, for ye have robbed me, even this whole nation." Too often many of us look forward to pay day and in the paying of bills and making purchases for ourselves, that we forget to give back to God the tenth which is his. Then again, sometimes we put aside God's money but when we find ourselves running short, we borrow from God and most often, can never repay it. I have experienced the latter.

It took a Sabbath morning in church for a member to reveal how God's blessings came in abundance once he paid his tithes and offering. Having listened to him, I realized I had nothing to lose but hopefully something to gain if I gave it a try. You see, I was one who could not bear for a bill to not be paid in full. So, from time to time, I 'borrowed' from my tithes in the hopes of replacing the money the next month. There were times I was able to replace the funds, but most times I was not. However, I decided to test the testimony shared.

Would you believe I found the testimony to be true? In fact, I found it to work instantly? In maintaining my new commitment and not borrowing from the tithes, there was insufficient money to pay at least one of my bills in full. However, I found that somehow when the due date came around money appeared. Surprisingly, money that had been borrowed from me and that I had written off and had long forgotten was repaid or former students would see me and just give money to treat myself to lunch. Of course they gave me more than I would spend on lunch and I would have just enough to make up the balance needed. Having had this wonderful experience and knowing that ten percent of money given to us is not ours to begin with, I ensure that my tithes and offerings are paid and in full. As a result, fifteen percent of my salary goes to God each month – ten percent tithes and five percent offering. Since then, I have never found myself worrying over a bill. I have learnt to put my finances in God's hand and allow Him to work it out and indeed He does.

As I reflect on my forty-seven years on this earth, there is no doubt that I have been blessed. I have had a wonderful and fulfilling and rewarding experience as a teacher. Just recently, I was given the post of principal on the island of San Salvador. Yet another blessing extended to me.

I have had the opportunity to teach, counsel and serve as a principal, all over a spread of twenty-five years. All of my successes thus far and no doubt those still to come, are and will be as a result of the God's goodness.

God does so much for us even when we are undeserving of his goodness. Despite our shortcomings and the disappointments we send His way, He continues to forgive us and comes to our aid. Do you want to experience the goodness of God in your life? If you do, I encourage you to develop a relationship with Him, believe in Him, trust in Him, worship Him and place your life in his hand. I guarantee you that once you do; you will be amazed at the working of God in your life.